Words
From The
Honeycomb

by

Hilly Kendrick

Grosvenor House

All rights reserved
Copyright © Hilly Kendrick, 2015

The right of Hilly Kendrick to be identified as the author of this work has been asserted by her in accordance with Section 78 of the Copyright, Designs and Patents Act 1988

The book cover picture is copyright to Petr Kratochvil

This book is published by
Grosvenor House Publishing Ltd
28-30 High Street, Guildford, Surrey, GU1 3EL.
www.grosvenorhousepublishing.co.uk

This book is sold subject to the conditions that it shall not, by way of trade or otherwise, be lent, resold, hired out or otherwise circulated without the author's or publisher's prior consent in any form of binding or cover other than that in which it is published and without a similar condition including this condition being imposed on the subsequent purchaser.

A CIP record for this book
is available from the British Library

ISBN 978-1-78148-925-3

I have known Hilly most of my adult life but her love of poetry goes further back than that. She started writing poetry while she was at secondary school and has never lost her love for the written word. I have watched her grow and blossom as a person and a poet. Her words touch every human emotion and I hope the readers of her book will gain joy and inspiration from her poetry ... Suz

"Pleasant words are like a honeycomb, sweetness to the soul and health to the bones."

Proverbs 16:24

My thanks to -
my teachers who inspired and encouraged me,
dear friends and family,
and lastly to God, who brought me here in the first place.

Contents

1. A Child Is Born — 1
2. A Jar of Love — 2
3. A Life Divine — 3
4. Alpha and Omega — 6
5. Always Hope — 7
6. Always There — 8
7. As One Our Church — 11
8. Before and After… — 12
9. Believe — 13
10. Captain of My Heart — 16
11. Carpenter — 17
12. Celebrate this Day — 18
13. Close to Heaven — 21
14. Cornerstone — 22
15. Faith, Hope, Truth – Our Journey — 23
16. Fall From Grace — 26
17. Gate of New Beginnings — 27
18. Hearts on Fire For God — 28
19. Herodias (The Plan) — 31
20. His Garden — 32
21. His Rain — 33
22. His Sacrifice — 36
23. I Know — 37
24. Incomparable — 38
25. Journey of Hands — 42
26. Just Knock — 43
27. Key to Life — 44
28. Mary's Lullaby — 47
29. Mothering Sunday — 48
30. New Life — 49

31.	Oh Lord…	52
32.	Palm Sunday	53
33.	Protector (Sweet Little Prince)	54
34.	Remember Him	57
35.	Risen!	58
36.	Salvation	59
37.	See	62
38.	Silent Traveller	63
39.	The Betrayed and the Betrayer	64
40.	The Gift of Hope	67
41.	The Gifts of the Holy Spirit	68
42.	The Hymn of Christ	69
43.	The Lamb	72
44.	The Light and the Longing – Mary Magdalene	73
45.	The One	75
46.	The Power of Prayer	78
47.	The Quiet Revolution	79
48.	Things to Do	80
49.	Who We Are – A Celebration	83
50.	You	84
51.	You Make Me Smile	85

A Child Is Born

What marvellous gentle babe is this, who lies upon a straw filled bed?
Small eyes stare up into the night; a thousand stars adorn his head.
Oh welcome, welcome everyone, from the four corners of the earth,
come worship him and bring your gift, to celebrate the virgin birth.
A wondrous sight this tiny child, born in a stable so forlorn,
God's greatest gift has come at last; Lord Jesus Christ the child is born.
He has come down to save the world, to bring us hope, remove all pain,
He comes to save our wretched souls, yes; Jesus Christ has come to reign!
What marvellous gentle babe is this, who lies upon a bed of straw?
As loving eyes look fondly down, to ever worship and adore.

A Jar of Love

A jar of love will bring a smile, that's all it really takes,
to brighten and enlighten every friendly heart that aches.
A jar of love is something that will see you through the day,
to give your life true meaning, in a pure and gentle way.
A jar of love is kindness, which is such a joy to see,
a growing warmth within your soul, one glorious way to be.
A jar of love is all it takes, but so much more than this,
is when you're in God's garden, flowers greet you with a kiss.

A Life Divine

We give our thanks, oh gentle Christ,
proclaiming You throughout the earth,
raise thankful voices to the One,
for all His works from humble birth.
We glory in your holy name,
rejoicing with all those who seek
to fill their hearts with peace and love,
so many hang on words You speak.
You give us strength, You give us hope,
we seek the face that shows the way,
not to forget what He has done,
to keep the faith, not go astray.
We know we are His chosen ones,
and must adhere to Holy law,
for on that day that we are judged,
as generations went before.
His covenant has been confirmed,
we stand and wait, we stand in line,
no miracle just to believe,
more so to live a life divine.

My Thoughts

My Thoughts

Alpha and Omega

Upon the cross He died for us,
his love He would not hide from us,
and all the angels cried for us,
the day our dear Lord died.
Beneath the cross the soldiers fight,
cast lots upon His robes in spite,
believing that it was their right,
the day our dear Lord died.
The heavens wept, the sky turned grey,
so many faces turned away,
the faithful few kneeled down to pray,
the day our dear Lord died.
The shouting voice, the angry scorn,
his head pierced by the vicious thorn,
the temple curtains split and torn,
the day our dear Lord died.
He gave His life to save His sheep,
we must not mourn, we must not weep,
for he has saved us from the deep,
the day our dear Lord died.
Upon the cross he died for us,
his love He would not hide from us,
and all the angels cried for us,
the day our dear Lord died.

Always Hope

There's always hope, you've no need to despair,
just look toward our Lord and He is there,
to take your hand and whisper in your ear,
and guide you through all troubles without fear.

There's always hope, so don't you ever doubt,
you're human, it's okay to scream and shout,
a silence will return to calm your heart,
then on the morrow, make a brand new start

There's always hope, of that you can be sure,
our Lord is just there, waiting at the door,
one knock is all it takes to let Him in,
so easy, once you know how to begin.

There's always hope, you'll find it bound in love,
we have assurances from God above,
as long as we remember how to pray,
the hope He gives us, will not go away.

Always There

He is here upon my waking, gets me up to face the day,
guides me through the good and bad times, He will never go away.
He is with me through the daytime, when I'm walking through the town,
always there to keep me going, if things start to drag me down.
He is there upon my pillow, in my head while fast asleep,
all His words my heart will treasure, His dear love I'll always keep.

My Thoughts

My Thoughts

As One Our Church

When good friends are drawn together,
hearts are lifted up in song,
there's a sense of true commitment,
and a feeling you belong.
Honest love born out of friendship,
lasts a lifetime we all know,
stronger links which bind us closer,
like a seed we watched it grow.
Our excited voices mingle,
with perhaps a hug or two,
and that timeless sound of laughter,
swapping stories old and new.
When good friends are brought together,
it's the best it's ever been,
just recounting all the good times,
everything you've done and seen.
And the silent cord that binds us,
grows more tight with every word,
intermingled with God's music,
it's the best you ever heard.
Here we have a home so peaceful,
we are one as friend to friend,
but far better, that dear Angel,
who is with us to the end.
When good friends are come together,
underneath God's blessed sky,
we all know there'll be a next time,
even though we say goodbye.

Before and After...

Before I was a Christian everything seemed cut and dried,
I didn't go to church much; that is true.
My life just ambled onward, an uncomplicated ride,
with nothing in my world 'cept me and you.

But then a crisis happened that affected both our lives,
you just decided one night, we should go
down to the church, where it is said, religious freedom strives,
to calm the heart where troubled waters flow.

A welcome we were given, by a small and happy band,
a strange relief swept over you and I.
Was it the song or prayer that spoke, the feel of a warm hand?
There was a peacefulness you can't deny.

I cried Remembrance Sunday for the loss of many souls,
but then I thought about another man.
Two thousand years ago he gave his life for the whole world,
I realise now we all were in his plan.

Believe

*Easter is not just about
cuddly bunnies, fluffy chicks
and chocolate eggs,
it is about one man
who sacrificed Himself
took on our sin
so that we could learn
to walk in His shadow,
love one another,
believe.*

*After Easter
the cuddly toys are put away,
the chocolate egg
eaten in a blink of an eye
and Jesus?
Please don't put Him away too
His life lives on in us
His word stays in our hearts
He is always here,
believe.*

My Thoughts

My Thoughts

Captain of My Heart

He is there upon the blue horizon, always close and never out of reach,
He's a starfish playing in the ocean; He's a pebble resting on a beach.
He has set our finale destination, an oasis way up in the sky,
It's an island some have called Salvation, and it waits in peace for you and I.
He has planned our course in perfect detail; He has known this from the very start,
He is strong and at the helm forever and I know He's the captain of my heart.
I believe He's the captain of my heart.

Carpenter

The hands lie limp beside His form,
a silence reigns to quell the storm,
His soul has gone to Father's care,
soon to return and make repair.
Carpenters hands they used to be,
a child who had a destiny,
now lay a sleeping in His tomb,
returning to His Fathers womb.

Now far away from all His pain,
all wounds restored, He'll rise again.

Celebrate this Day

Blackbird song awoke me to the dawn,
misty-eyed I welcomed in the morn,
granted yet another day to live,
thanking God for all that He can give.
Every day a blessing, this I know,
He is watching me where 'ere I go,
great creator of the earth and sky,
marvels to behold in my mind's eye.
Bless You for this day You freely give,
granting me another day to live.

My Thoughts

My Thoughts

Close to Heaven

My face is aching from the cold, I cannot feel my nose,
my ears have turned to deepest pink, except for all my toes.
We had the most amazing walk, my little friend and I,
where fields go on forever, melting into bluest sky.

I thought to take the Common Road, the locals had a hand,
they recommended I should try, a change from sea and sand.
How right they were, how pleased was I, to find such peaceful bliss,
Tall windmills stood in silence, frosty winds gave me a kiss.

A steady crunching underfoot we headed to the sun,
and all the while beside me walked my little fluffy one.
She longed to jump into the ditch that held the frozen brine,
but I thought better of it than to let her off the line.

So many birds in busy song were chattering in the cold,
my steps were steady, true and strong, my little one so bold.
I thought about the warmer months, the changing of the view,
With lighter clothes and sunny smiles, so many walks to do.

I felt that close to heaven, as I stood and waved goodbye,
where fields went on forever, melting into bluest sky.

Cornerstone

My soul finds rest in God alone,
he is my rock, my cornerstone.
When I feel lost and torn apart,
he sets things right inside this heart.
And sometimes when I lose my way,
for from life's path I often stray,
I know He's there to shine a light,
I take His hand and hold on tight.
I feel His eyes upon me now,
as I write down each treasured vow,
to keep the faith as best I know,
to follow Him where He may go.
He helps me up each time I fall,
his love wraps round me like a shawl.
He takes away my doubt – defeat,
gives strength whatever ills entreat.
I look up at the glorious sky,
I know He's there just standing by.
And when I glance down at the earth
I see in nature His re-birth.
His words lift up my tired heart,
they show me how to play my part.
My hand in His will ever be,
he is my rock eternally.
And in that deepest darkest place,
I hear His voice, I see His face.
My soul finds rest in God alone,
he is my rock, my cornerstone.

Faith, Hope, Truth – Our Journey

'Oh ye of little faith' is said, we hear it often – pages read,
but, if we trust our living God, our feet will lead where others trod.
Far from a leap into the dark our faith sheds light upon our path,
to trust in God opens the door, and we pass through as those before.
Faith like the wind cannot be seen, but it is there, has always been,
believe and speak it if you dare, it isn't easy but it's there.

'Hope springs eternal' is the phrase; hold onto it throughout your days,
hope knows no fear and we may fall, where there is life then hope is all.
To not have hope what can life bring? Our hearts are robbed of everything,
hope is an anchor for the soul, when angry waves can take their toll.
Hold on to hope, do not give in, and you will see new life begin,
as from a little tiny seed, hope springs eternal – the strong reed.

We hear that 'truth will set you free' and so it will as we will see,
it is the armour we must wear, repel the lies that rip and tear.
Our God is truth as truth itself, and we must seek it, know its stealth,
truth is the source of faith and hope, as we ascend each dangerous slope.
Faith, hope and truth, the three main things, used by so many – even kings,
we kneel to make the solemn vow, our journey is beginning now.

My Thoughts

My Thoughts

Fall From Grace

A war broke out in heaven, between Lucifer and God,
with pride and envy heading up the list.
The story is that Lucifer, a follower of Satan,
desired to be as God, this dark snake hissed.

A heart filled with desire intense and pride too much to bear,
an angel not created out of sin.
But only when creation reached fulfilment, he rebelled,
an evil heart of joy watched war begin.

The highest of all angels, though it's thought, not of the good,
but chieftain of the rebel angels too.
His aura was a magnet to those angels fall from grace,
and so his rebel army did accrue.

They retained all natural knowledge, their angelic intellect,
but through their veins flowed sin, as thick as oil.
Inflexible and obstinate, these unrepentant souls,
one aim in life, to ruin and despoil.

Somehow I feel a sorrow for these angels fall from grace,
for they will never find a perfect peace.
Although despite their efforts, to draw men to wicked ways,
the glory of God's power will never cease.

Wherever they do battle with the hearts and minds of men,
besetting those on earth who still resist.
They always carry with them punishment, the pains of hell,
to add yet more lost souls upon the list.

They turned away from God; in doing this they lost the fight,
while angelic souls in heaven rule above them day and night.

Gate of New Beginnings

There's a gate of new beginnings and it's just around
    the bend,
only takes a few short steps and then you're there.
It's a place I visit often, like a faithful dear old friend,
and the sun is always shining everywhere.

You can listen to a blackbird, busy building up its nest,
or the rustling sound of leaves, tossed in the breeze.
Very early in the morning is the time I like the best,
just before new petals open to the bees.

I can sit alone forever, though, not really on my own,
for so many things surround me when I'm here.
Gaze across the lush green farmland, where a new seed has
    been sown,
It's amazing how the colours change each year.

Let me take you where the air is filled with blossom scent
    so rare,
every day is filled with magic, end to end.
We don't have to talk, just listen, as the wind plays in
    our hair,
by the gate of new beginnings, time to spend.

Hearts on Fire For God

Celebrate the Holy Spirit which descends upon us all,
as true followers of Jesus, we respond to every call.
For today within this chapel birthday blessings do abound,
life refreshed, a new beginning, listen to the joyful sound!
Coming with the warmth of summer, hear it in the
    mighty wind,
hail this day of confirmation, flames protect all who
    have sinned.
Rescued from the depths of darkness, love reigns now strong
    and supreme,
trusting Christ our true salvation, life assured, this is
    no dream.
Such great changes in the lost heart, faith in Christ brings
    hope anew,
sin has lost it's hold forever, now believing what is true.
* "The best of all is God is with us", there beside us
    should we fall,
God's grace is a gift accept it, *"Free in all and free for all"!

(*quotes from Wesley)

My Thoughts

My Thoughts

Herodias (The Plan)

Herodias brings forth the head, of one who was beloved of God,
her daughter's dance had sealed his fate, while fingers clicked
   and bare feet trod.
A cold black heart filled with revenge, intent on carrying out
   her plan,
defy her husband Antipas and kill a long imprisoned man.

For Antipas thought on the words, that John the Baptist
   preached to those
who had become his followers, and thus we read, the Gospel
   shows.
With prompting from her mother, so determined now to have
   her way,
Salome shed her veils for him, to celebrate his birthing day.

Within his cell, the Baptist prayed and put his trust in God the
   Son,
while up above his head, a Queen, in triumph smiled for she
   had won.
Poor Antipas was so entranced, by his young daughter's
   swaying hips,
his mind ran wild and he cried out, 'What just reward?' from
   quivering lips.

Herodias once more pressed hard, resolved to make her
   daughter say –
'Bring me the head of him you keep, in chains of iron' – she
   had her way.
Thus Antipas could not refuse, although within his heart was fear,
he had not wanted this to be, but what he had to do was clear.

The deed was done, the charger brought, on which there lay
   the preacher's head,
Herodias, now satisfied, God's prophet John the Baptist, dead.

His Garden

*The beauty of a garden is tender loving care,
and every bud and flower has golden joy to share.
When busy bees come calling their treasure for to seek,
they land upon each petal and gently take a peek.*

*The beauty of a garden – however mad this world,
is just to sit a minute and watch a dream unfurled.
We know that He is sitting quite close in gentle peace,
just watching us and waiting as new born flowers increase.*

*The beauty of a garden is such a joy to share,
but better far than all things is knowing God is there.*

His Rain

Sweet blessed rain you fall as tears upon my thankful face,
thus christening my ears, my eyes, my lips with perfect grace.
Cold droplets decorate my hair; they shiver in the breeze,
my heart is full of love and joy, no winter wind could freeze.

I watch the colours of the clouds that travel overhead,
a magic ballerina act, who knows where they are led?
Old coat wrapped tight against the spray, I laugh into the sky,
my skin is cleansed a thousand times, a thousand times
    You cry.

I dodge the puddles down the lane; each one reflects a cloud,
young leaves drip wet with new-born rain, all cobwebs are
    a shroud.
No sun to stop our reverie, no rainbow to embrace,
just You and I together, tracing raindrops down my face.

My Thoughts

My Thoughts

His Sacrifice

He gave His life for us, that we might live,
to follow in the steps He left behind.
Profess our love, all enemies forgive,
to open eyes belonging to the blind.

He took our sin, a burden great to bear,
our souls were cleansed, all thought of evil dead.
So we must learn to banish greed and share,
drink from His cup, with reverence, break the bread.

A place awaits us beyond heaven's gate,
we must continue in His way to love.
we do not know how long we have to wait,
but He is watching always from above.

Enfold His wandering sheep, the weak and blind.
take up the cross, bear witness and forgive.
We follow in the steps He left behind,
He gave His life for us, that we might live.

I Know

*I know You will not turn away this heart
that keeps You here within its secret place.
I am aware how I must play my part,
and feel a thankful smile upon my face.*

*I know You will not take away this love
I give so freely in Your sacred name.
As pure and white the ever present dove,
will always be as true the very same.*

*I know You will forever live in me,
keep me secure upon this troubled earth.
With prayer and song forever living free,
I give to You as much as I am worth.*

*I know that You will guide me through this life,
with all the peaks and troughs it seems to throw.
To follow You until the end of days,
wherever You will lead me I will go.*

Incomparable

*There is nothing to compare a silent walk through russet
     leaves,
when your friends are busy birds and scudding cloud.
And the scent of pine and wood smoke, envelope your shape
     and weaves
a mysterious web of camouflage hung shroud.*

*With the sounds of Mother Nature wafting in and out
     the trees,
my feet move through the soft carpet, without sound.
I decided long ago that there is none compares with these,
all the magic life created in the ground.*

*Such serenity I have felt while on my walks through wooded
     glades,
hand in hand I go with blackbird song and dove.
Young grey squirrels bounce from branches, sending leaves
     in rich cascades,
while the sun brings warmth and light from up above.*

*With the sounds of Mother Nature dancing up and through
     the trees,
my heart floats above the mass that clothes the ground.
I decided long ago that there is none compares with these,
all the wonders of the universe now found.*

*You are here inside my head as I walk on towards the light,
where the trees give way to sky, for just a while.
I am plunged back into day as I emerge from darkest night,
welcome sunshine hits my face, I start to smile.*

*With the sounds of Mother Nature playing tunes in aged
    oak trees,
my feet move as in a trance upon the ground.
I decided long ago that there is none compares with these,
the most dearest treasures, safe within the ground.*

*Fronds of bracken brush my leg, the sweetest dew melts
    on my face,
let me stay in here forever and become one with this place.*

My Thoughts

My Thoughts

Journey of Hands

His hands fashioned rough oak in earlier days
the Holy Spirit filled His soul
His hands began their journey
to wave and to beckon
resting upon heads of lost souls
of those needing to be healed
hands that gently gathered wandering flocks
broke bread and poured wine
shared peace and love
came together in fervent prayer
finally broken with nails
such tender loving hands
did not deserve such an end
but with the end came a new beginning
so that now we can lift up OUR hands
and rejoice
give thanks for His hands
that touched and healed us.

Just Knock

There is always hope for those who lose their way,
that one door is waiting to be knocked,
all lost souls are welcomed,
His door is never locked.

There is always time to have another try,
that one door is waiting to be knocked,
no one is forgotten,
His door is never locked.

There is always love to give a straying sheep,
that one door is waiting to be knocked,
Saviour to the missing,
His door is never locked.

There is always hope for those if they believe,
that one door is waiting to be knocked,
you can be forgiven,
His door is never locked.

Key to Life

*The key that unlocks many doors,
so must you choose which way to go,
before you even think to turn,
the one thing that all life can show.*

*To summon courage and go forth,
and seek what you believe is true,
open the door to firm belief,
discover what is inside you.*

*The open door invites you through,
the key is cool inside your palm,
as onward goes the road before,
welcome new life and gentle calm.*

My Thoughts

My Thoughts

Mary's Lullaby

Angel among angels, lying softly in my arms,
silent in your dreaming, I sing to you my psalm of psalms –
Dearest little one, little one...
Sleeping in a manger, with the oxen standing by,
stars out in their thousands, they decorate a velvet sky –
For you my little one, little one...
Hands so soft and tiny, yet a power so divine,
highest heaven adores you; I can't believe that you are mine.
Dearest little one, little one...
Angel among angels, lying softly in my arms,
silent in your dreaming, I sing to you my psalm of psalms –
Oh my little one, dearest little one....

Mothering Sunday

*Early morning walks are good for the soul,
you can watch the sun wake up, yawn,
stretch her warm arms.*

*My faithful little friend plods on beside me
noticing nothing – except
new smells and foxes.*

*Birds are up and busy, how they chatter.
Curtains remain drawn,
how can they miss this?*

*I smile up at the sky and whisper –
'It's alright…'*

*Early morning walks are good for the soul,
they help dry tears that still need to sleep.*

New Life

The stone is moved, the Lamb is free,
He's born again for you and me,
all evil vanquished, good has won,
a brand new life has just begun.
Now, pushed away the stone that sealed,
at last three spirits now revealed,
oh, blessed be our God on high,
enthroned the Son none can deny.
They did not take Him far away,
good people, He is here to stay,
archangels are protecting Him,
with all His grace filled to the brim.
Sing praises – our Redeemer lives,
He gave us life and still forgives!

My Thoughts

My Thoughts

Oh Lord...

Oh Lord when you look down upon this earth that
    You created,
how can it be that peace and love became so underrated?
So many things that have gone wrong,
I know I must have faith, keep strong.

There is such evil in this world and still we do not listen,
the barren lands the bleeding wounds, in many eyes
    tears glisten.
So many times we lose our way,
so many times we need to pray.

Corrupted hearts and misled minds, the banners waved
    in hatred,
how can it be true feelings have become so understated?
So many things that have gone wrong,
I know I must have faith, keep strong.

And yet there is some goodness if we seek beneath
    the darkness,
revealing that deep down inside, it's there despite
    the starkness.
So many times we lose our way,
so many times we need to pray.

Oh Lord You gave your only Son to turn us from our sinning,
we throw it all back in your face, go back to the beginning.
We know at times we have gone wrong,
we'll keep the faith, we will be strong.
Although at times we lose our way,
we'll kneel in silent thanks and pray.

Oh gentle God reveal in us the love that is inside us,
we do believe, we will keep faith, for You are here to guide us.

Palm Sunday

They waved their palms, the frantic fickle hoard,
they cried 'Hosanna! Blessed is the Lord!'
A man upon a donkey, with one thought,
to save those wretched souls who cared for nought.

Palm branches scattered, carpeting the ground,
but on he rode, not speaking, not one sound.
And still the crowds, their voices ringing out,
'Blessed is the King of Israel!' – Who could doubt?

Within the week, those voices would deny,
'Give us Barabbas, Jesus crucify!'
They balled their fists, this frantic fickle hoard,
betrayed the sweetest Lamb, our dearest Lord.

A man upon a donkey, with one thought,
to save those wretched souls who cared for nought.

Protector (Sweet Little Prince)

Protect you I promise my sweet little Prince,
from evils which threaten your sacred small life.
By God I was chosen, my sweet little Prince,
bring peace to this world, put an end to all strife.

True Virgin of God, I have vowed to keep safe,
my dearest, my own I will nurture with care.
My sweeting, my precious, I vow to keep safe,
far into the future, His sweet love we'll share.

Gaze gently upon Him, my sweet little Prince,
whom I have brought forth to becalm stormy seas.
Give thanks to our God for my sweet little Prince,
look up to the heavens and fall to your knees.

My Thoughts

My Thoughts

Remember Him

We break the bread remembering,
He gave His body for our sin,
nailed to a cross of rough-hewn wood,
vanquished all evil saved the good.
In drinking wine we do confirm,
belief in Christ from whom we learn,
He shed His blood so we might live,
love one another and forgive.

Risen!

*The tombstone has been rolled away,
warm sun awakes a brand new day,
rejoice with thankful hearts and say,
our Lord is risen now!
Upon the cross was crucified,
eternal life, He has not died,
to bring us hope, long been denied,
our Lord is risen now!
We cast aside all dark despair,
He is amongst us, everywhere,
to bless and give His special care,
Our Lord is risen now!
With joyful hearts we sing out loud,
we throw away death's heavy shroud,
let us join hands, stand up, be proud,
our Lord is risen now!*

Salvation

*Nobody knows when our Lord will return,
not even God Himself.
But He will come like a thief in the night,
moving with powerful stealth.
Darkness will fall on the ones who break free,
the light will surround those who stay,
never to live in the blackness of night,
secure in God's love they will lay.
We must be watchful not give way to sleep,
ready ourselves for the day,
put on the armour that bears faith and love,
steeling ourselves for the fray.
Salvation's helmet sits firm on our head,
through God this treasure awaits,
He sacrificed all so that we might survive,
to pass through the eternal gates.
Nobody knows when our Lord will come back,
to gather His lost wandering sheep,
some will break free, maybe go their own way,
others will enter His keep.*

*Greet true salvation like welcoming sun,
we must all strive to continue as one.*

My Thoughts

My Thoughts

See

To see Him is to see life everlasting,
to dwell within His heart,
to live beneath His love,
to know He is our shield,
just close your eyes.

Just close your eyes to see
the wonder of His strength,
the beauty of His face,
the truth in His eyes,
He is always with you.

He is always with you
to the very end,
to hold your hand,
to lead you to safety,
guiding you to paradise.

Guiding you to paradise,
He is always with you,
just close your eyes,
to see Him is to see life everlasting,
Amen.

Silent Traveller

A donkey went travelling' o'er desert and hill,
the night sky a blanket, the air was so still.
His burden was precious, the sweet Mary maid,
he moved oh so gently, each kind word obeyed.

With nothing but water and no star to guide,
the woman his burden, a man walks beside.
To Bethlehem city they would make their way,
where a stable was waiting with a manger of hay.

A small silent traveller with a cross on his back,
must carry his treasure and keep on the track.
A dangerous journey, a long way to go,
with a dear fragile maiden, her head hung so low.

A star lit the place where the baby did lay,
it shone out for miles and it showed all the way.
The shepherds, a donkey and all living things,
a baby in a manger and worshipping kings.

A donkey went travelling' through a street laid with palms,
so far from sweet Mary, her safe loving arms.
The throng cried 'Hosanna! Make way for the king!'
One day they would know of the hope He would bring.

The Betrayed and the Betrayer

He was betrayed by one corrupt and lost,
for thirty silver pieces, such a cost.
The heart that Satan stole would never rest,
a rope hung from a tree, the final test.

He was betrayed by those who loved Him too,
they would deny all that He said was true.
A cock would crow three times He prophesied,
confronted by the mob, faith sought to hide.

He was betrayed by those who knew Him not,
His words of love and wisdom soon forgot.
Great temples torn asunder at His death,
our sin cast out within a single breath.

We all betrayed a pure and gentle heart,
whose love was given freely from the start.
Through sacrifice He did redeem us all,
believe we must and wait upon His call.

The thirty coins were cursed, this much we know,
used for a land where seed refused to grow.
In fields of Haceldama all has died,
within the Bible this was prophesied.

My Thoughts

My Thoughts

The Gift of Hope

There is a hope that calms life's storms,
that quells the doubt, sustains the heart.
I put my hope in You oh God,
all other things I set apart.

Authority and power are yours,
and that is why we look to You.
You light the path when we are lost,
then point the way to what is true.

Remind me of your goodness Lord,
oh yes – you're there in clouds above.
Whenever I feel uninspired,
You let me rest within your love.

I put my hope in God alone,
all other things I set apart.
There is a hope that calms life's storms,
it quells the doubt, sustains the heart.

The Gifts of the Holy Spirit

How lucky that we have the choice, to live and act the way we do,
our Lord has given us a voice and so we practice what is true.
With wisdom we can bear all trials, help take the burden from our friends,
face up to all our self-denials, be patient for the gift God sends.
To understand the reason why, God placed us on this wondrous earth,
where oceans heave beneath blue sky and death concedes to life and birth.
We counsel deep within our heart when troubles threaten to disrupt,
our faith is sometimes torn apart, but nothing can God's love corrupt.
He gave us strength to rise above adversity, now ground to dust;
true fortitude becomes a dove, replacing all with faith and trust.
The gift of knowledge helps us see what right or wrong path we might take,
temptation says it holds the key, at times bad judgements we can make.
To please our Lord in all we do, show piety to those who serve,
instils in us a love so true and from His path we must not swerve.
For we were made by only Him, who taught us love through gentle ways,
He will not let our faith grow dim; we follow all the length of days.
As we love those who love us too, we find there is the gift of choice,
and so we practice what is true; our Lord has given us a voice.

The Hymn of Christ

My life is no shadow like you I was born,
and so my arms open to you the ripe corn.
My eyes can see through you embracing your mind,
I open my arms to all those who are blind.
My feet they are bathed with your sorrowful tears,
I open my arms to your worries and fears.
My spirit is yours to keep close and to hold,
I open my arms to the young and the old.

Come take my hand, touch now my side,
pain I have known and so you have cried.
Drink of my wine; eat of my bread,
for this is my body, which for you once bled.

God is your true cornerstone, you has He made,
thus with fervent prayer your doubts are allayed.
Live not in the shadows and be not dismayed,
come into the sunshine, run free from the shade.
The path may be hard, at times riddled with fear,
but never forget, in your heart I am here.
My love is for all, I say, take it and share,
you open your arms to me, I'm always there.

My Thoughts

My Thoughts

The Lamb

Alone He pushed the evil hand away,
throughout the lonely night was left to pray,
when all about Him fell into repose,
His blood began to fall as red as rose.

Strong soul to keep the faith and stand His ground,
where ignorance and selfishness abound,
a gentle soul whose heart was free from sin,
would later in that day arise and win.

I worship and adore this Man of Peace,
and pray that worldwide suffering might cease,
we kneel before the One who shows the way,
toward the light that opens up the day.

The Light and the Longing – Mary Magdalene

She was a soul tormented, for too long had been abused,
a woman lost, not knowing who she was.
Within a stranger's walls all hope of gentle love refused,
abandoned in the dark, alone because –
her innocence long taken with a heart once more betrayed,
found cornered by a mob who screamed their hate.
All chances of escaping very soon began to fade,
the crowd increased in strength, alas too late.
But who is this that cuts a swathe and rises up His hand,
to charge those who would cast the cowardly stone?
He kneels and with His finger traces lines into the sand.
How is it she no longer feels alone?
She wondered why the mob had dropped their stones
     and backed away,
looked up to see a face well-worn with care.
He lifts her from the dust and brings her safely into day,
and pushes from her eyes dishevelled hair.
'Go, sin no more' He says, but Mary could not comprehend,
the people had all shrunk away in fear.
Could this be really happening had this man become
     her friend?
Maybe the light she longed for was right here?
So she followed Him and listened, learning more and more
     each day,
and over time her other self was shed.
A new life lay before her, longing much to know the way,
she hung on every word her master said.
Imagine then, when suddenly cruel people stole her 'light',
the one good person she had learnt to trust.
Remembering those moments she discovered what was right,
remembering that finger in the dust.
His tomb was cold and empty but through tears she saw
     a man,

He spoke her name, she could not move away.
A light so strong, a face in brightness, difficult to scan,
but then all was revealed upon that day.
Discovering her 'Rabboni' was alive – no longer dead,
now risen and it brought such pure delight.
Her heart was full to bursting; words in thousands filled
   her head,
the longing to believe returned her light.

The One

You taught us to forgive and then showed us how to love,
we look to You for guidance sent down from up above,
the rules are not so difficult as every Christian knows,
just loving one another and then watching how love grows.
You opened up Your arms to all unbelieving hoards,
who ignorant of love could only hate and draw their swords,
You healed the weak and helpless with the power in Your hands,
and spread all love and mercy running rivers through the land.
You are our only Saviour the true one and only Lord,
together we stand firm and strong bound tightly by Your cord,
We know You will be waiting at the gates of paradise,
we realise dear master for our sins You paid the price.

My Thoughts

My Thoughts

The Power of Prayer

*There's a special gift we're given, meant for everyone to share,
something precious to believe in, called the blessed power
of prayer.*

*When you feel defeated, saddened, by a world that
doesn't care,
bring your worries to our Father; try the blessed power
of prayer.*

*If the dark skies cloud your heaven, and it feels like no
one's there,
you will find your missing sunshine, with the blessed power
of prayer.*

*God will let you do the talking, pour a cup, pull up a chair,
He will always sit and listen, to the message in your prayer.*

*Just be still and feel His presence, for our Lord is everywhere,
He will take on all your troubles, through the blessed power
of prayer.*

The Quiet Revolution

We start by being joyful – it's the only way to go,
and as we read the message, we learn to seek, to grow.
Continually praying, giving every bit of thanks,
the quiet revolution won't resort to guns and tanks.

All prophecies are tested, seek only what is good,
to follow the true Master the only way we should.
His will is placed before us; we feel the spirit's fire,
the quiet revolution repels all bad desire.

The peace we find is sanctified, in body and in mind,
remember, we are fallible, to His children God is kind.
Just hold on to the goodness, keep from you what is bad,
the quiet revolution gives the hope you never had.

As John preceded Jesus, proclaiming who would come,
we will keep on believing in God's almighty Son.
At His coming we'll be ready, with our faith to keep
*   us strong,*
for the quiet revolution will establish right from wrong.

To turn the cheek in silence and offer just our hand,
it's up to those who take it, with God's love – understand.
He is the one and only, the reason that we live,
the quiet revolution is the way we must forgive.

Things to Do

*I hear the busy chatter of the cleaners in the church,
arranging flowers and polishing the pews.
My eyes appraise the furnishings, a silent wandering search,
as gentle voices echo all their news.*

*So here I sit and think of those who live inside this heart,
and gaze upon a window's rainbow stain.
I find deep comfort in this place, so close and yet apart,
a peace and solace from a world insane.*

*I know He listens to my prayers and gently holds my hand,
His voice is but a whisper in my ear.
I watch the candles flicker on the simple alter stand,
while conscious of the happy chatter near.*

*I come and sit here many times in contemplative thought,
as gentle souls work hard upon their chores.
But time will nudge me on and there are many things to sort,
like ironing shirts and washing paw streaked floors.*

My Thoughts

My Thoughts

Who We Are – A Celebration

How good to live in unity, our God is gracious to us all,
His face shines down on everyone, and in our hearts we hear
His call.
His ways span the whole universe, we lift our voices, sing
our praise,
the harvest will be plentiful, and in our hearts we know
His ways.
For we are part of all He made, uniquely fashioned one
by one,
as perfect as the stars and moon, as warm and bright as
summer sun.

Our ears hear birdsong, crashing wave, our eyes watch every
season change,
our skin feels cooling wind and rain, our lives a constant
rearrange.
To smell fresh lavender and rose, to taste the fruits our earth
supplies,
we thank our God for who we are, we celebrate the sea
and skies.
I marvel at the velvet night and try to count each myriad star,
and in my heart I celebrate and thank our God for who
we are.

You

You are our treasure, the only true joy,
constant and patient and hard to annoy.
You are the sky, and the glorious sun,
that's why we call You the heavenly one.
You are the flowers, a fragrance so sweet,
gentle spring showers, refreshing, complete.
You are for always my faithful dear friend,
only on your love my faith can depend.
You are a snowflake, so small, white and pure,
when I am ailing You give me the cure.
You give me hope when all troubles confound,
putting me back on the merry-go-round.
You fit the pieces that make up my life,
matching together as husband to wife.
You are the angel, who watches at night,
gentle warm winds on a flickering light.
You are the ground, restless waves on the sea,
life-giving oxygen, rushing and free.
You are the pilgrim, who brings me good news,
solving each mystery, You hold the clues.
You stand beside me and help me to try,
You never rest in the earth, sea or sky.
You are the passion I hold in these eyes,
upholding truthfulness, defeating lies.
You are the river, in which we all flow,
where You have ventured we have yet to go.
You will return staying true to your vow,
embracing all with the love You endow.

You Make Me Smile

Who chases dark clouds, when they come closing in,
who makes me feel so happy in my skin?
Who wakes the flowers to brighten for a while?
I know it's true just because You make me smile.

You bring me the sun and the blue sky up above,
You make me smile.
Gently take my hand and You keep me safe in your love-
You make me smile.
For I know, I'll always walk with You
through the bad times and the good –
because I love You so,
and the simple reason that I do –
You make me smile.

Raindrops fall softly, as they dance upon my face,
I'm lost in your wonderful time and space.
Who paints the rainbows to brighten for a while?
I know it's true just because You make me smile.

For You keep me from all danger,
and You guard my heart at night.
You can never be a stranger,
I can feel your power and might.

You bring me the sun and the blue sky up above,
You make me smile.
Gently take my hand and You keep me safe in your love –
You make me smile.
For I know, I'll always walk with You,
through the bad times and the good –
because I love You so,
and the simple reason that I do –
You make me smile.

My Thoughts

My Thoughts